SLOW FASHION
made fast

LEISURE ARTS, INC. • Maumelle, Arkansas

With the growing push for social responsibility and conscious consumerism, younger generations are finding a passion for age-old crafts like knitting that allow them to create mindful, special pieces for themselves and loved ones.

Slow fashion has become a trend amoung today's population and with it an interest in DIY fashionable, wearable pieces. The modern maker wants more sophisticated items that they can wear and gift with pride, and they need quick projects to fit into their busy schedule.

From the meditative and cognitive benefits of the practice to the appreciation of the finished product, hand making garments and accessories is a healthful addiction for the mind and spirit. This book provides instructions for 12 fashion forward accessories, garments, and home décor items, all at the skill level of an advanced beginner. With easy techniques and simple shapes, and projects ranging from a weeknight to a weekend's commitment, you will be inspired to take your skills to the next level.

Each project was thoughtfully chosen with the maker in mind. These pieces are inspired by classic favorites and designed with Lion Brand® Wool-Ease Thick & Quick® yarn to fly off your needles. As soon as you bind off one pattern, you'll want to cast on the next.

Alexandra Tavel is a knitwear designer based in New York City, designing under her label Two of Wands.

With a passion for handcrafted knits, Alexandra launched Two of Wands in 2014. Her designs were an immediate breakout success, being sought out by international customers and boutiques. She has since designed for Vogue Knitting Magazine, Lion Brand Yarn, DMC Thread, and numerous others. Her knitting and crochet patterns can be found on multiple platforms including her site, www.twoofwands.com.

Hailing from a small town in the Midwest taught Alexandra the importance of designing approachable, practical pieces, but living in NYC and traveling around the world gives her great inspiration to design unique and stylish items at the same time. Her style is chic but playful and pulls inspiration from nature, history, trends, and function.

Combining influences from experience with cut-and-sew garments, draping, and jewelry making, she strives to design special pieces with simple but unexpected details. Her design process starts with a feeling – a moment in time that she wants to capture with a garment or accessory.

Alexandra graduated from Indiana University with a BA in Fashion Design and an AA in Costume Construction Technology. She has been living and working in New York City for over a decade.

contents

latvian braid COWL

SHOPPING LIST

Yarn (Super Bulky Weight)

[6 ounces, 106 yards
(170 grams, 97 meters) per skein**]**:

- ☐ Color A (Grey) - 2 skeins
- ☐ Color B (Off White) - 1 skein
- ☐ Color C (Black) - 1 skein

Knitting Needle

24" (61 cm) Circular,

- ☐ Size 15 (10 mm)
  or size needed for gauge

GAUGE INFORMATION

In Stockinette Stitch (knit every rnd),
8.5 sts and 13 rnds = 4" (10 cm)

Note: Cowl is worked in the round.

EASY

Finished Size:
16" high x 24½" circumference
(40.5 cm x 62 cm)

COWL

With Color A, cast on 52 sts; being careful **not** to twist sts, place marker to indicate the beginning of the rnd ***(see Markers, page 28, and Using A Circular Needle, page 60)***.

Rnd 1 (Right side)**:** Purl around.

Rnd 2: Knit around.

Rnd 3: Purl around.

Rnds 4 and 5: Repeat Rnds 2 and 3.

Rnds 6-12: Knit around.

Do **not** cut Color A; drop Color A to **wrong** side of work.

Right Leaning Latvian Braid

Rnd 13: ★ K1 with Color B, K1 with Color C; repeat from ★ around.

Bring **both** yarns, Color B and Color C to the **right** side (front) of work.

Rnd 14: Crossing the new color **under** the previous color to work each st, ★ P1 with Color B, P1 with Color C; repeat from ★ around.

Colors B and C will become very twisted on this round, but will untwist on the following round. Keep floats loose to prevent puckering.

Rnd 15: Crossing the new color **over** the previous color to work each st, ★ P1 with Color B, P1 with Color C; repeat from ★ around.

Cut Colors B and C and continue with Color A.

Rnds 16-26: Knit around.

Do **not** cut Color A; drop Color A to **wrong** side of work.

Left Leaning Latvian Braid

Rnd 27: ★ K1 with Color B, K1 with Color C; repeat from ★ around.

Bring **both** yarns, Color B and Color C to the **right** side (front) of work.

Rnd 28: Crossing the new color **over** the previous color to work each st, ★ P1 with Color B, P1 with Color C; repeat from ★ around.

Rnd 29: Crossing the new color **under** the previous color to work each st, ★ P1 with Color B, P1 with Color C; repeat from ★ around.

Cut Colors B and C and continue with Color A.

Rnds 30-40: Knit around.

Right Leaning Latvian Braid

Rnd 41: ★ K1 with Color B, K1 with Color C; repeat from ★ around.

Bring **both** yarns, Color B and Color C to the **right** side (front) of work.

Rnd 42: Crossing the new color **under** the previous color to work each st, ★ P1 with Color B, P1 with Color C; repeat from ★ around.

Rnd 43: Crossing the new color **over** the previous color to work each st, ★ P1 with Color B, P1 with Color C; repeat from ★ around.

Cut Colors B and C and continue with Color A.

Rnds 44-50: Knit around.

Rnd 51: Purl around.

Rnd 52: Knit around.

Rnd 53: Purl around.

Rnds 54 and 55: Repeat Rnds 52 and 53.

Bind off loosely in **knit**.

blanket BASKET

SHOPPING LIST

Yarn (Super Bulky Weight) SUPER BULKY 6
[6 ounces, 106 yards
(170 grams, 97 meters) per skein]:
☐ 3 skeins

Knitting Needle
29" Circular,
☐ Size 17 (12.75 mm)
or size needed for gauge

Additional Supplies
☐ Stitch marker

GAUGE INFORMATION

With two strands held together,
in Stockinette Stitch
(knit one row, purl one row),
6.5 sts and 9 rows = 4" (10 cm)
In basket weave pattern
(Rnds 1-8 of Sides),
one repeat (8 sts) = 5" (12.75 cm);
8 rnds = 3¼" (8.25 cm)

●●○○ **EASY**

Finished Measurements:
10" square x 7" high
(25.5 cm x 18 cm)

Notes: Basket begins with a square base, then stitches are picked up all the way around the edges of the square and worked in the round from the bottom up. Two strands of yarn are held together throughout. To do so, pull the inner end out from the center of the skein and hold together with the outer end.

BASE

With two strands held together, cast on 18 sts.

Row 1 (Right side)**:** Knit across.

Row 2: Purl across.

Rows 3-25: Repeat Rows 1 and 2, 11 times; then repeat Row 1 once **more**.

Do **not** bind off.

SIDES

Foundation Rnd: With **right** side facing and working in end of rows, pick up 18 sts evenly spaced across left side of Base ***(Figs. 10a & b, page 63)***; pick up 18 sts across cast on edge; working in end of rows, pick up 18 sts evenly spaced across right side of Base; place marker to indicate the beginning of the rnd ***(see Markers, page 58, and Using A Circular Needle, page 60)***: 72 sts.

Rnd 1 (Right side)**:** Knit around.

Rnds 2-4: (P5, K3) around.

Rnd 5: Knit around.

Rnds 6-8: P1, K3, (P5, K3) around to last 4 sts, P4.

Rnds 9-17: Repeat Rnds 1-8 once, then repeat Rnd 1 once **more**.

Bind off all sts in **knit**.

eyelet striped WRAP

SHOPPING LIST

Yarn (Super Bulky Weight) SUPER BULKY 6

[6 ounces, 106 yards (170 grams, 97 meters) per skein]:

- ☐ 4 skeins

Knitting Needle

32" (81 cm) Circular,

- ☐ Size 15 (10 mm) **or** size needed for gauge

Additional Supplies

- ☐ Stitch markers

GAUGE INFORMATION

In Garter Stitch (knit every row),
8 sts and 15 rows = 4" (10 cm)

TECHNIQUES USED

- YO *(Fig. 4, page 61)*
- K2 tog *(Fig. 6, page 62)*

●●○○ EASY

Finished Measurements:
69" wide (wingspan) x 25½" high
(175.5 cm x 65 cm)

Notes: Wrap is worked from the top down, increasing 4 stitches on every other row. The bound off edge forms the outer V-shaped sides, making it is important to bind off **loosely** to prevent this edge from pulling and to allow it to drape nicely.

WRAP

Cast on 7 sts.

Row 1: K1, YO, K2, YO, pm, K1, pm, YO, K2, YO, K1: 11 sts.

Row 2 AND ALL EVEN NUMBERED ROWS: Knit across slipping markers as you come to them.

Row 3: K1, YO, knit across to next marker, YO, sm, K1, sm, YO, knit across to last st, YO, K1: 15 sts.

Row 5 (Increase row)**:** K1, YO, K1, (YO, K2 tog) across to within one st of next marker, K1, YO, sm, K1, sm, YO, K1, (K2 tog, YO) across to last 2 sts, K1, YO, K1: 19 sts.

Rows 7-20: Repeat Rows 5 and 6, 7 times: 47 sts.

Row 21 (Increase row)**:** K1, YO, knit across to next marker, YO, sm, K1, sm, YO, knit across to last st, YO, K1: 51 sts.

Rows 23-26: Repeat Rows 21 and 22 twice: 59 sts.

Row 27 (Increase row)**:** K1, YO, K1, (YO, K2 tog) across to within one st of next marker, K1, YO, sm, K1, sm, YO, K1, (K2 tog, YO) across to last 2 sts, K1, YO, K1: 63 sts.

Rows 29-50: Repeat Rows 27 and 28, 11 times: 107 sts.

Row 51 (Increase row)**:** K1, YO, knit across to next marker, YO, sm, K1, sm, YO, knit across to last st, YO, K1: 111 sts.

Rows 53-56: Repeat Rows 51 and 52 twice: 119 sts.

Row 57: K1, YO, K1, (YO, K2 tog) across to within one st of next marker, K1, YO, sm, K1, sm, YO, K1, (K2 tog, YO) across to last 2 sts, K1, YO, K1: 123 sts.

Rows 59-64: Repeat Rows 57 and 58, 3 times: 135 sts.

Row 65 (Increase row)**:** K1, YO, knit across to next marker, YO, sm, K1, sm, YO, knit across to last st, YO, K1: 139 sts.

Rows 67-70: Repeat Rows 65 and 66 twice: 147 sts.

Row 71 (Increase row)**:** K1, YO, K1, (YO, K2 tog) across to within one st of next marker, K1, YO, sm, K1, sm, YO, K1, (K2 tog, YO) across to last 2 sts, K1, YO, K1: 151 sts.

Rows 73-78: Repeat Rows 71 and 72, 3 times: 163 sts.

Bind off all sts loosely in **knit**.

Tassels

Make 3 Tassels ***(Figs. 12a & b, page 63)***, using twenty 14" (35.5 cm) lengths of yarn per tassel.

Tie the tassels onto the 3 corners of the wrap and knot to secure.

wall HANGING

SHOPPING LIST

Yarn (Super Bulky Weight) SUPER BULKY 6
[6 ounces, 106 yards
(170 grams, 97 meters) per skein]:
- ☐ 1 skein

Knitting Needles
- ☐ Size 15 (10 mm)
  or size needed for gauge

Additional Supplies
- ☐ 8 mm diameter Dowel rod - 24" (61 cm) length
- ☐ Yarn needle
- ☐ Crochet hook (for fringe)

GAUGE INFORMATION

In Garter Stitch (knit every row),
8.5 sts and 15 rows = 4" (10 cm)
In pattern, one repeat
(14 sts) = 5" (12.75 cm)

TECHNIQUES USED

- YO *(**Fig. 4, page 61**)*
- K2 tog *(**Fig. 6, page 62**)*
- SSK *(**Figs. 8a-c, page 62**)*
- Slip 2 tog, K1, P2SSO *(**Figs. 9a & b, page 62**)*

●●○○ **EASY**

Finished Size:
15" wide x 18" long (38 cm x 45.5 cm)
(excluding fringe)

Notes: Wall hanging is worked from the bottom up. Instead of binding off, the live stitches are slipped onto the dowel rod. Fringe is added once work is complete.

BODY

Cast on 43 sts.

Row 1 (Right side)**:** K1, ★ YO, K5, slip 2 tog, K1, P2SSO, K5, YO, K1; repeat from ★ 2 times **more**.

Row 2: Knit across.

Repeat Rows 1 and 2 until piece measures approximately 14" (35.5 cm) from cast on edge, ending by working a **knit** row.

Next Row: K1, ★ YO, K2 tog, K9, SSK, YO, K1; repeat from ★ 2 times **more**.

Next Row: Knit across.

Next 4 Rows: Repeat last 2 rows twice.

Do **not** bind off; cut yarn.

Transfer sts onto a scrap piece of yarn. Secure and weave in all ends.
Block work to expand the stitches a little and prevent puckering; then slip sts from scrap yarn onto dowel rod.

Cut a 30" (76 cm) length of yarn and tie onto each end of dowel rod to create a hanger.

Cut twenty-six 12" (30.5 cm) lengths of yarn and separate into 13 groups of two strands each.

Using photo as a guide for placement, add groups of fringe across bottom edge ***(Figs. 11a & b, page 63)***.

moss cocoon CARDIGAN

SHOPPING LIST

Yarn (Super Bulky Weight)

[6 ounces, 106 yards
(170 grams, 97 meters) per skein]:

☐ 7 skeins

Knitting Needles

16" (40.5 cm) **and**
40" (101.5 cm) Circular,

☐ Size 15 (10 mm)
or size needed for gauge

Additional Supplies

☐ Stitch marker

☐ Yarn needle

GAUGE INFORMATION

In pattern,
9 sts and 12 rows = 4" (10 cm)

●●○○ **EASY**

Finished Measurements:
40" wide (cuff to cuff) x 38" high
(101.5 cm x 96.5 cm)

Notes: Cardi is worked flat in moss stitch as a large rectangle, which is then folded and seamed from the bottom edge up on either side, leaving space for armholes. Body and cuff edging is picked up and knit in stockinette in the round.

BODY

With longer needle, cast on 90 sts.

Rows 1 and 2: (K1, P1) across.

Rows 3 and 4: (P1, K1) across.

Repeat Rows 1-4 for pattern until piece measures approximately 36" (91.5 cm) from cast on edge.

Bind off all sts in pattern.

Fold rectangle so that the bound off edge meets the cast on edge and rectangle is approximately 40" (101.5 cm) wide by 18" (45.5 cm) tall with the fold at the top.
Seam sides together from the bottom edge up approximately 10" (25.5 cm), leaving an 8" (20.5 cm) opening for armholes.

EDGING

Body

With **right** side facing and using longer needle, pick up sts ***(Fig. 10b, page 63)*** in each st around entire Body (cast on and bound off edge); place marker to indicate the beginning of the rnd ***(see Markers, page 58, and Using A Circular Needle, page 60)***.

Rnds 1-12: Knit around.

Bind off all sts loosely in **knit**.

Armhole

With **right** side facing and using shorter needle, pick up sts ***(Fig. 10a, page 63)*** evenly around one Armhole edge (approximately 3 sts for every 4 rows); place marker to indicate the beginning of the rnd.

Rnds 1-8: Knit around.

Bind off all sts loosely in **knit**.

Repeat around second Armhole edge.

crisscross cable PONCHO

SHOPPING LIST

Yarn (Super Bulky Weight) SUPER BULKY 6

[6 ounces, 106 yards
(170 grams, 97 meters) per skein]:

- ☐ 5 skeins

Knitting Needle

24" (61 cm) Circular,

- ☐ Size 15 (10 mm)
  or size needed for gauge

Additional Supplies

- ☐ Cable needle
- ☐ Yarn needle
- ☐ Crochet hook (for fringe)

GAUGE INFORMATION

In Stockinette Stitch
(knit one row, purl one row),
8.5 sts and 13 rows = 4" (10 cm)

●●○○ **EASY**

Finished Measurements:
32" wide x 24" long (to point)
(81.5 cm x 61 cm)

Notes: Poncho is worked flat in two panels which are seamed together to form Poncho. Neckband is then picked up and knit in the round.

STITCH GUIDE

CABLE 4 BACK ***(abbreviated C4B)***
(uses next 4 sts)
Slip next 2 sts onto cable needle and hold in **back** of the work, K2 from left needle, K2 from cable needle.

CABLE 4 FRONT ***(abbreviated C4F)***
(uses next 4 sts)
Slip next 2 sts onto cable needle and hold in **front** of the work, K2 from left needle, K2 from cable needle.

CABLE 6 BACK ***(abbreviated C6B)***
(uses next 6 sts)
Slip next 3 sts onto cable needle and hold in **back** of the work, K3 from left needle, K3 from cable needle.

CABLE 6 FRONT ***(abbreviated C6F)***
(uses next 6 sts)
Slip next 3 sts onto cable needle and hold in **front** of the work, K3 from left needle, K3 from cable needle.

PANEL (Make 2)

Cast on 36 sts.

Row 1 (Right side)**:** K1, P2, K4, P2, K1, P2, K 12, P2, K1, P2, K4, P2, K1.

Row 2 AND ALL WRONG SIDE ROWS: P1, K2, P4, K2, P1, K2, P 12, K2, P1, K2, P4, K2, P1.

Row 3: K1, P2, K4, P2, K1, P2, K 12, P2, K1, P2, K4, P2, K1.

Row 5: K1, P2, C4B, P2, K1, P2, K 12, P2, K1, P2, C4F, P2, K1.

Row 7: K1, P2, K4, P2, K1, P2, C6B, C6F, P2, K1, P2, K4, P2, K1.

Row 9: K1, P2, K4, P2, K1, P2, K 12, P2, K1, P2, K4, P2, K1.

Row 11: K1, P2, C4B, P2, K1, P2, K 12, P2, K1, P2, C4F, P2, K1.

Row 13: K1, P2, K4, P2, K1, P2, K 12, P2, K1, P2, K4, P2, K1.

Row 15: K1, P2, K4, P2, K1, P2, K 12, P2, K1, P2, K4, P2, K1.

Row 17: K1, P2, C4B, P2, K1, P2, C6B, C6F, P2, K1, P2, C4F, P2, K1.

Row 19: K1, P2, K4, P2, K1, P2, K 12, P2, K1, P2, K4, P2, K1.

Row 21: K1, P2, K4, P2, K1, P2, K 12, P2, K1, P2, K4, P2, K1.

Row 23: K1, P2, C4B, P2, K1, P2, K 12, P2, K1, P2, C4F, P2, K1.

Row 25: K1, P2, K4, P2, K1, P2, K 12, P2, K1, P2, K4, P2, K1.

Row 27: K1, P2, K4, P2, K1, P2, C6B, C6F, P2, K1, P2, K4, P2, K1.

Row 29: K1, P2, C4B, P2, K1, P2, K 12, P2, K1, P2, C4F, P2, K1.

Row 30: P1, K2, P4, K2, P1, K2, P 12, K2, P1, K2, P4, K2, P1.

Rows 31-92: Repeat Rows 1-30 twice, then repeat Rows 1 and 2 once **more**.

Bind off all sts in pattern.

FINISHING

Block panels to 16" (40.5 cm) wide.

Using diagram below as a guide, sew bound off edge of first Panel to bottom right edge of second Panel at a right angle.

Sew bound off edge of second Panel to bottom right edge of first Panel at a right angle.

Neckband

With **right** side facing and working in end of rows, pick up an even number of sts around neckline (approximately 2 sts for every 3 rows) ***(Fig. 10a, page 63)***; place marker to indicate the beginning of the rnd ***(see Markers, page 58, and Using A Circular Needle, page 60)***.

Rnds 1-5: (K1, P1) around.

Bind off all sts loosely in pattern.

Fringe

Cut seventy-two 12" (30 cm) lengths of yarn and separate into 18 groups of four strands each.

Add 9 groups of fringe evenly spaced across the cast on edges of each panel ***(Figs. 11a & b, page 63)***.

Trim fringe to desired length.

DIAGRAM

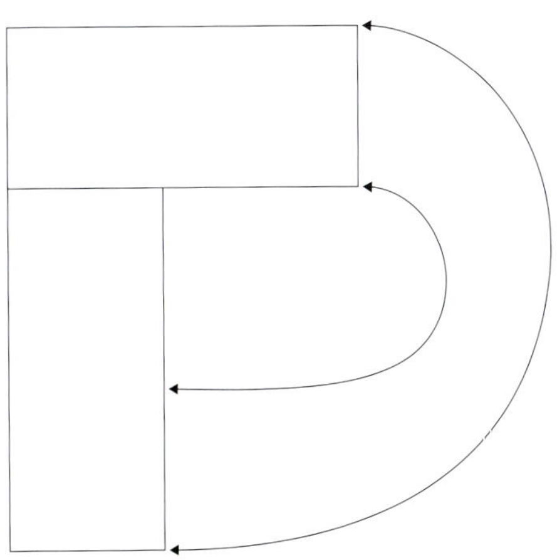

garter pyramid BLANKET

SHOPPING LIST

Yarn (Super Bulky Weight) SUPER BULKY 6
[6 ounces, 106 yards
(170 grams, 97 meters) per skein]:
☐ 4 skeins

Knitting Needle
29" (74 cm) Circular,
☐ Size 19 (15 mm)
or size needed for gauge

GAUGE INFORMATION

In Stockinette Stitch
(knit one row, purl one row),
7 sts and 9 rows = 4" (10 cm)

●●○○ **EASY**

Finished Measurements:
40" wide x 44" long
(101.5 cm x 112 cm)

Notes: Blanket is worked flat from end to end. Side borders are picked up and knit once blanket is complete.

BLANKET

Cast on 59 sts.

Rows 1-7: Knit across.

Row 8: Purl across.

Row 9 (Right side)**:** Knit across.

Row 10: P3, (K 11, P3) across.

Row 11: K4, P9, (K5, P9) across to last 4 sts, K4.

Row 12: P5, K7, (P7, K7) across to last 5 sts, P5.

Row 13: K6, P5, (K4, P1, K4, P5) across to last 6 sts, K6.

Row 14: P7, K3, (P4, K3) across to last 7 sts, P7.

Row 15: K8, P1, (K4, P5, K4, P1) across to last 8 sts, K8.

Row 16: P 12, K7, (P7, K7) twice, P 12.

Row 17: K 11, P9, (K5, P9) twice, K 11.

Row 18: P 10, K 11, (P3, K 11) twice, P 10.

Rows 19-92: Repeat Rows 7-18, 6 times; then repeat Rows 7 and 8 once **more**.

Rows 93-98: Knit across.

Bind off all sts in **knit**.

Side Border

With **right** side facing and working in end of rows, pick up 75 sts (approximately 3 sts per every 4 rows) evenly spaced across one side of Blanket ***(Fig. 10a, page 63)***.

Rows 1-6: Knit across.

Bind off all sts in **knit**.

Repeat across opposite side of Blanket.

Tassels

Make 10 Tassels ***(Figs. 12a & b, page 63)***, using sixty 14" (35.5 cm) lengths of yarn per tassel and wrapping a 12" (30.5 cm) length 2" (5 cm) below the top.

Tie 5 Tassels **each** evenly spaced across the cast on edge and bound off edge.

twist front HEADBAND

SHOPPING LIST

Yarn (Super Bulky Weight) SUPER BULKY 6
[6 ounces, 106 yards
(170 grams, 97 meters) per skein]:
☐ 4 skeins

Knitting Needles
☐ Size 15 (10 mm)
or size needed for gauge

Additional Supplies
☐ Yarn needle

GAUGE INFORMATION

In Stockinette Stitch
(knit one row, purl one row),
8 sts and 12 rows = 4" (10 cm)

●●○○ **EASY**

Finished Measurements:
7" wide x 19" circumference
(18 cm x 48.5 cm)

Note: Headband is worked in one piece and seamed at the front.

HEADBAND

Leaving a long end for sewing, cast on 14 sts.

Row 1 (Right side)**:** Knit across.

Row 2: Purl across.

Repeat Rows 1 and 2 until piece measures approximately 19" (48.5 cm) from cast on edge.

Bind off all sts in pattern, leaving a long end for sewing.

Fold bound off edge in half (wrong side together) and sew the first and last 5 sts together, leaving the center 4 sts un-sewn at the fold to create a hole. Bring one corner of the cast on edge through this hole from the right side, and sew the first and last 5 sts of the cast on edge together in the same manner as the bind off edge, interlocking the ends.

linen SCARF

SHOPPING LIST

Yarn (Super Bulky Weight) SUPER BULKY 6

[6 ounces, 106 yards
(170 grams, 97 meters) per skein]:

- ☐ Color A (Grey) - 2 skeins

[5 ounces, 87 yards
(140 grams, 80 meters) per skein]:

- ☐ Color B (Marble) - 2 skeins

Knitting Needles

- ☐ Size 15 (10 mm)
  or size needed for gauge

Additional Supplies

- ☐ Crochet hook (for fringe)

GAUGE INFORMATION

In pattern,
10 sts and 18 rows = 4" (10 cm)

●●○○ **EASY**

Finished Measurements:
11½" wide x 70" long
(29 cm x 178 cm)

Notes: Scarf is worked from end to end. All stitches are slipped purlwise. Twisted fringe is added once scarf is complete.

SCARF

With Color A, cast on 29 sts.

Row 1 (Right side)**:** K1, (slip 1 wyif, K1) across.

Row 2: P2, slip 1 wyib, (P1, slip 1 wyib) across to last 2 sts, P2.

Row 3: With Color B, K1, (slip 1 wyif, K1) across.

Row 4: P2, slip 1 wyib, (P1, slip 1 wyib) across to last 2 sts, P2.

Row 5: With Color A, K1, (slip 1 wyif, K1) across.

Repeat Rows 2-5 for pattern until piece measures approximately 70" (178 cm) from cast on edge, ending by working Row 2; cut Color B.

Bind off all sts in **knit**.

Cut thirty 20" (51 cm) lengths **each** of Colors A and B. Holding one strand of each color together, add fifteen 2-strand groups to each short end of Scarf ***(Figs. 11a & b, page 63)***.

Separate strands in half, holding both strands of each color together.

Twist both groups **tightly** in one direction separately until they begin to kink, then twist them together in the opposite direction so that they wrap around each other to form a rope.
Tie an overhand knot at the end.
Trim ends evenly.

loopy PILLOWCASE

SHOPPING LIST

Yarn (Super Bulky Weight) SUPER BULKY 6

[6 ounces, 106 yards
(170 grams, 97 meters) per skein]:

☐ 4 skeins

Knitting Needles

☐ Size 15 (10 mm)
or size needed for gauge

Additional Supplies

☐ 18" (45.5 cm) Square throw pillow
☐ Yarn needle

GAUGE INFORMATION

In Stockinette Stitch
(knit one row, purl one row),
8.5 sts and 13 rows = 4" (10 cm)

●●○○ **EASY**

Finished Size:
18" (45.5 cm) square

Notes: Pillowcase is shaped like an envelope to allow for easy insertion and removal of a throw pillow. Pattern is worked in one piece and begins with a ribbed edge and a stockinette portion, then the loopy front portion is knit, and it ends with the second stockinette portion and ribbed edge. Work is then folded like an envelope, overlapping the stockinette portions, and seamed up the sides.
Tug on loops every few rows of the loopy portion to tighten and secure them.

STITCH GUIDE

MAKE LOOP (uses one st)
Knit the next st but do **not** remove it from the left needle. Bring the working yarn **forward** between the needles and wrap it around the thumb of your left hand. Take the working yarn **back** between the needles and knit the **same** st again, this time removing it from the left needle. Pass the first st formed on the right needle over the second st to lock the loop in place.

BODY

Cast on 38 sts.

Rows 1-6: (K1, P1) across.

Row 7 (Right side)**:** Knit across.

Row 8: Purl across.

Repeat Rows 7 and 8 until work measures approximately 12" (30.5 cm) from cast on edge, ending by working a **purl** row.

Next Row: K1, make loop in each st across to last st, K1.

Next Row: Purl across.

Repeat the last 2 rows until loopy portion measures approximately 18" (45.5 cm), ending by working a **purl** row.

Next Row: Knit across.

Next Row: Purl across.

Repeat the last 2 rows until the Stockinette Stitch portion measures approximately 10" (25.5 cm), ending by working a **purl** row.

Next 6 Rows: (K1, P1) across.

Bind off all sts in pattern.

With **wrong** side facing, fold one stockinette/rib section up so that the **wrong** sides are together and the stockinette/rib section covers approximately 2/3 of the back of the loopy portion. Fold the second stockinette/rib portion so that it overlaps the first and forms an envelope to insert the pillow, again covering approximately 2/3 of the back of the loopy portion.

Sew the side seams.

ribbed TAM

SHOPPING LIST

Yarn (Super Bulky Weight) SUPER BULKY 6
[6 ounces, 106 yards
(170 grams, 97 meters) per skein]:
☐ 1 skein

Knitting Needles
16" (41 cm) Circular **and**
Double-pointed (set of 5),
☐ Size 15 (10 mm)
or size needed for gauge

Additional Supplies
☐ Stitch marker
☐ Yarn needle

GAUGE INFORMATION

In Garter Stitch
(knit one round, purl one round),
8 sts and 15 rnds = 4" (10 cm)

TECHNIQUES USED

- kfb ***(Figs. 5a & b, page 61)***
- K2 tog ***(Fig. 6, page 62)***
- P2 tog ***(Fig. 7, page 62)***

●●○○ **EASY**

Finished Measurements:
8½" high x 20" circumference
(21.5 cm x 51 cm)

Note: Tam is worked in the round.

TAM

Cast on 40 sts; being careful **not** to twist sts, place marker to indicate the beginning of the rnd ***(see Markers, page 58, and Using A Circular Needle, page 60)***.

Rnd 1 (Right side)**:** Knit around.

Rnd 2: Purl around.

Rnds 3 and 4: Repeat Rnds 1 and 2.

Rnd 5: ★ K1, kfb, K2, kfb; repeat from ★ around: 56 sts.

Rnds 6-21: (P3, K1) around.

Shaping

Change to double-pointed needles when there are too few stitches to use a circular needle ***(see Double-Pointed Needles, page 60)***.

Rnd 1: ★ P1, P2 tog, K1; repeat from ★ around: 42 sts.

Rnd 2: (P2, K1) around.

Rnd 3: (P2 tog, K1) around: 28 sts.

Rnd 4: (P1, K1) around.

Rnd 5: K2 tog around: 14 sts.

Cut yarn leaving a 12" (30.5 cm) length for sewing.

Thread yarn needle with long end and slip sts onto yarn needle; gather **tightly** to close and secure end.

Make a 3½-4" (9-10 cm) pom-pom and sew to top of Tam ***(Figs. 13a-c, page 64)***.

slouchy TOTE

SHOPPING LIST

Yarn (Super Bulky Weight)
[5 ounces, 87 yards
(140 grams, 80 meters) per skein]:
☐ 3 skeins

Knitting Needles
24" (61 cm) Circular **and**
Double-Pointed (set of 5),
☐ Size 15 (10 mm)
or size needed for gauge

Additional Supplies
☐ Stitch marker
☐ Yarn needle

GAUGE INFORMATION
In pattern,
10 sts and 18 rnds = 4" (10cm)

TECHNIQUES USED
- Adding New Sts ***(Figs. 3a & b, page 61)***
- Slip 2 tog, K1, P2SSO ***(Figs. 9a & b, page 62)***

●●○○ **EASY**

Finished Size: 15" wide x 18" high
(38 cm x 45.5 cm)

Notes: Bag is worked from the top down, first on circular needles and then on double-pointed needles as the number of stitches decreases. All stitches are slipped **purlwise** with yarn in front.

TOTE

Cast on 81 sts; being careful **not** to twist sts, place marker to indicate the beginning of the rnd ***(see Markers, page 58, and Using A Circular Needle, page 60)***.

Rnd 1 (Right side)**:** K1, (slip 1 wyif, K1) around.

Rnd 2: Slip 1 wyif, (K1, slip 1 wyif) around.

Repeat Rnds 1 and 2 for pattern until piece measures approximately 3" (7.5 cm) from cast on edge, ending by working Rnd 2.

Next Rnd: (K1, slip 1 wyif) 9 times, bind off next 22 sts, slip 1 wyif, (K1, slip 1 wyif) 8 times, bind off next 22 sts: 37 sts.

Next Rnd: (Slip 1 wyif, K1) 9 times, **turn**; add on 22 sts, **turn**; (slip 1 wyif, K1) 9 times, **turn**; add on 22 sts, **turn**; slip 1 wyif: 81 sts.

Repeat Rnds 1 and 2 until piece measures approximately 16" (40.5 cm) from cast on edge, ending by working Rnd 2.

Shaping

Change to double-pointed needles when there are too few stitches to use a circular needle ***(see Double-Pointed Needles, page 60)***.

Rnd 1: K1, (slip 1 wyif, K1) 3 times, slip 2 tog, K1, P2SSO, K1, ★ (slip 1 wyif, K1) 8 times, slip 2, K1, P2SSO, K1; repeat from ★ 2 times **more**, (slip 1 wyif, K1) 5 times: 73 sts.

Rnd 2: Slip 1 wyif, (K1, slip 1 wyif) around.

Rnd 3: K1, (slip 1 wyif, K1) around.

Rnd 4: (Slip 1 wyif, K1) 3 times, slip 2, K1, P2SSO, ★ K1, (slip 1 wyif, K1) 7 times, slip 2, K1, P2SSO; repeat from ★ 2 times **more**, (K1, slip 1 wyif) 5 times: 65 sts.

Rnd 5: K1, (slip 1 wyif, K1) around.

Rnd 6: Slip 1 wyif, (K1, slip 1 wyif) around.

Rnd 7: K1, (slip 1 wyif, K1) twice, slip 2, K1, P2SSO, K1, ★ (slip 1 wyif, K1) 6 times, slip 2, K1, P2SSO, K1; repeat from ★ 2 times **more**, (slip 1 wyif, K1) 4 times: 57 sts.

Rnd 8: Slip 1 wyif, (K1, slip 1 wyif) around.

Rnd 9: K1, (slip 1 wyif, K1) around.

Rnd 10: (Slip 1 wyif, K1) twice, slip 2, K1, P2SSO, ★ K1, (slip 1 wyif, K1) 5 times, slip 2, K1, P2SSO; repeat from ★ 2 times more, (K1, slip 1 wyif) 4 times: 49 sts.

Rnd 11: K1, (slip 1 wyif, K1) around.

Rnd 12: Slip 1 wyif, (K1, slip 1 wyif) around.

Rnd 13: K1, slip 1 wyif, K1, slip 2, K1, P2SSO, K1, ★ (slip 1 wyif, K1) 4 times, slip 2, K1, P2SSO, K1; repeat from ★ 2 times **more**, (slip 1 wyif, K1) 3 times: 41 sts.

Rnd 14: Slip 1 wyif, ★ K1, slip 2, K1, P2SSO, (K1, slip 1 wyif) 3 times; repeat from ★ 3 times **more**: 33 sts.

Rnd 15: K1, ★ slip 2, K1, P2SSO, K1, (slip 1 wyif, K1) twice; repeat from ★ 3 times **more**: 25 sts.

Rnd 16: Slip 2, K1, P2SSO, ★ K1, slip 1 wyif, K1, skip 2, K1, P2SSO; repeat from ★ 2 times **more**, (K1, slip 1 wyif) twice: 17 sts.

Cut yarn leaving a 12" (30.5 cm) length for sewing.

Thread yarn needle with long end and slip sts onto yarn needle; gather **tightly** to close and secure end.

general INSTRUCTIONS

ABBREVIATIONS

C4B	Cable 4 Back
C6B	Cable 6 Back
C4F	Cable 4 Front
C6F	Cable 6 Front
cm	centimeters
K	knit
kfb	knit in front & back
mm	millimeters
P	purl
P2SSO	pass 2 slipped stitches over
pm	place marker
Rnd(s)	Round(s)
sm	slip marker
st(s)	stitch(es)
tog	together
wyib	with yarn in back
wyif	with yarn in front
YO	yarn over

SYMBOLS & TERMS

★ — work instructions following ★ as many **more** times as indicated in addition to the first time.

( ) or **[ ]** — work enclosed instructions **as many** times as specified by the number immediately following **or** contains explanatory remarks.

colon (:) — the number(s) given after a colon at the end of a row or round denote(s) the number of stitches you should have on that row or round.

GAUGE

Exact gauge is **essential** for proper size. Before beginning your project, make a sample swatch in the yarn and needles specified in the individual instructions. After completing the swatch, measure it, counting your stitches and rows or rounds carefully. If your swatch in larger or smaller than specified, **make another, changing needle size to get the correct gauge**. Keep trying until you find the size needles that will give you the specified gauge.

MARKERS

When using double-pointed or circular needles, a split-ring marker is placed around the first stitch of the round to indicate the beginning of a round. Place a marker as instructed and move it up at the beginning of each round.

KNIT TERMINOLOGY		
UNITED STATES		INTERNATIONAL
gauge	=	tension
bind off	=	cast off
yarn over (YO)	=	yarn forward (yfwd) **or** yarn around needle (yrn)

Yarn Weight Symbol & Names	LACE 0	SUPER FINE 1	FINE 2	LIGHT 3	MEDIUM 4	BULKY 5	SUPER BULKY 6	JUMBO 7
Type of Yarns in Category	Fingering, size 10 crochet thread	Sock, Fingering, Baby	Sport, Baby	DK, Light Worsted	Worsted, Afghan, Aran	Chunky, Craft, Rug	Super Bulky, Roving	Jumbo, Roving
Knit Gauge Ranges in Stockinette St to 4" (10 cm)	33-40 sts**	27-32 sts	23-26 sts	21-24 sts	16-20 sts	12-15 sts	7-11 sts	6 sts and fewer
Advised Needle Size Range	000 to 1	1 to 3	3 to 5	5 to 7	7 to 9	9 to11	11 to 17	17 and larger

* GUIDELINES ONLY: The chart above reflects the most commonly used gauges and needle sizes for specific yarn categories.

** Lace weight yarns are usually knitted on larger needles to create lacy openwork patterns. Accordingly, a gauge range is difficult to determine. Always follow the gauge stated in your pattern.

●○○○ **BASIC**	Projects using basic stitches. May include basic increases and decreases.
●●○○ **EASY**	Projects may include simple stitch patterns, color work, and/or shaping.
●●●○ **INTERMEDIATE**	Projects may include involved stitch patterns, color work, and/or shaping.
●●●● **COMPLEX**	Projects may include complex stitch patterns, color work, and/or shaping using a variety of techniques and stitches simultaneously.

KNITTING NEEDLES																		
U.S.	0	1	2	3	4	5	6	7	8	9	10	10½	11	13	15	17	19	35	50
U.K.	13	12	11	10	9	8	7	6	5	4	3	2	1	00	000	---	---	---	---
Metric - mm	2	2.25	2.75	3.25	3.5	3.75	4	4.5	5	5.5	6	6.5	8	9	10	12.75	15	19	25

USING A CIRCULAR NEEDLE

When you knit a tube, you are going to work around on the outside of the circle, with the **right** side of the knitting facing you.

Using a circular needle, cast on all stitches as instructed. Untwist and straighten the stitches on the needle to be sure that the cast on ridge lies on the inside of the needle and never rolls around the needle.

Hold the needle so that the skein of yarn is attached to the stitch closest to the right hand point. Place a marker on the right hand point to mark the beginning of the round *(Fig. 1)*.

To begin working in the round, knit the stitches on the left point.

Continue working each round as instructed without turning the work.

Fig. 1

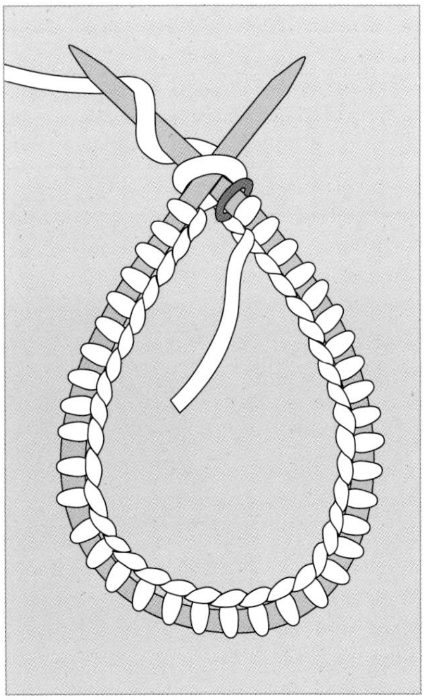

USING DOUBLE-POINTED NEEDLES

When working a piece that is too small to use a circular needle, double-pointed needles are required. Divide the stitches into fourths and slip one-fourth of the stitches onto each of 4 double-pointed needles ***(Fig. 2a)***, forming a square ***(Fig. 2b)***. Do **not** twist the cast on ridge. With the fifth needle, knit across the stitches on the first needle. You will now have an empty needle with which to knit the stitches from the next needle. Work the first stitch of each needle firmly to prevent gaps. Continue working around without turning the work.

Fig. 2

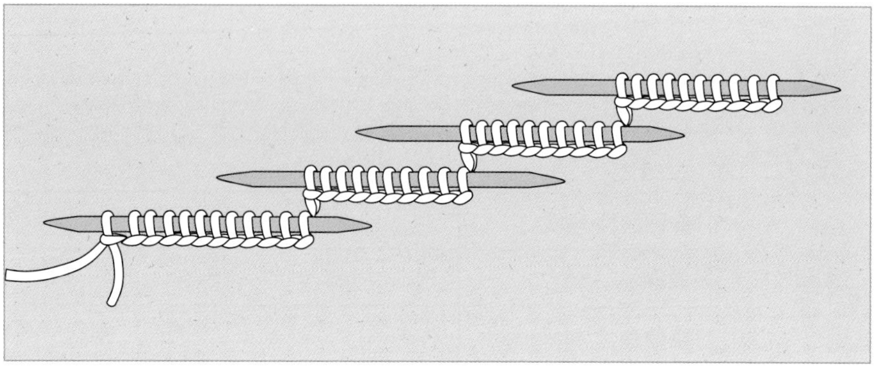

Fig. 2b

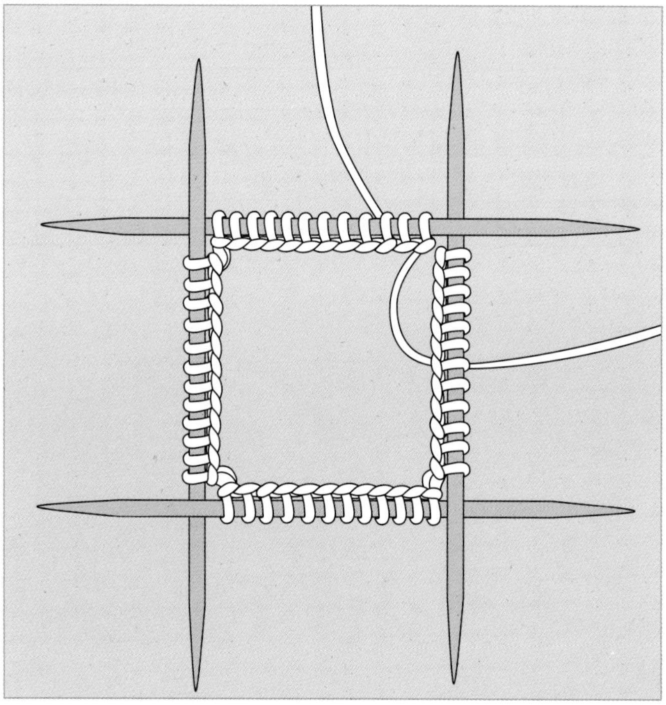

ADDING NEW STITCHES

Insert the right needle into the next stitch as if to **knit**, yarn over and pull loop through *(Fig. 3a)*, insert the left needle into the loop just worked from **front** to **back** and slip the loop onto the left needle *(Fig. 3b)*. Repeat for the required number of stitches.

Fig. 3a

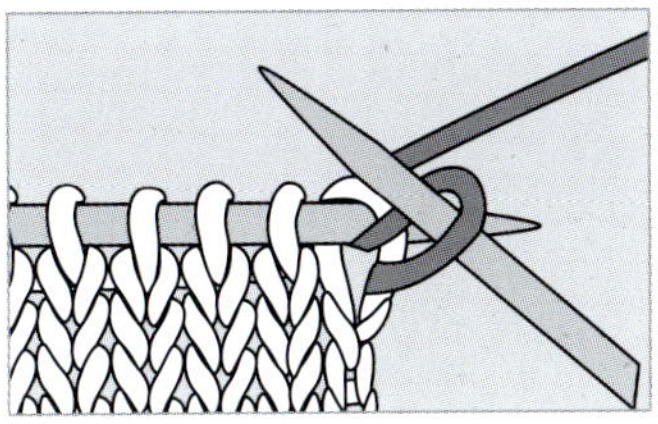

Fig. 3b

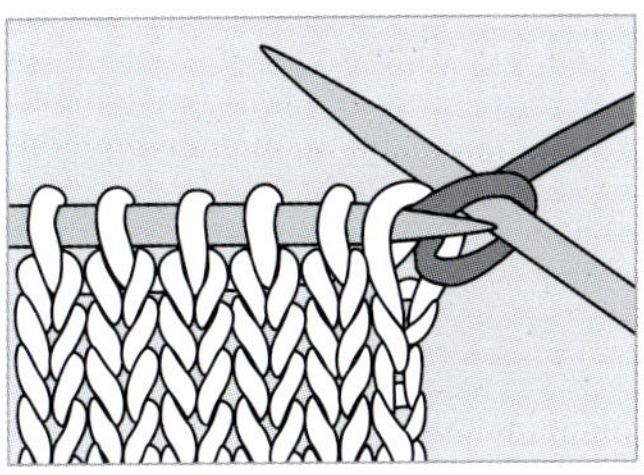

INCREASES

Yarn Over *(abbreviated YO)*

After a knit stitch, before a knit stitch

Bring the yarn forward **between** the needles, then back over the top of the right hand needle, so that it is now in the position to knit the next stitch *(Fig. 4)*.

Fig. 4

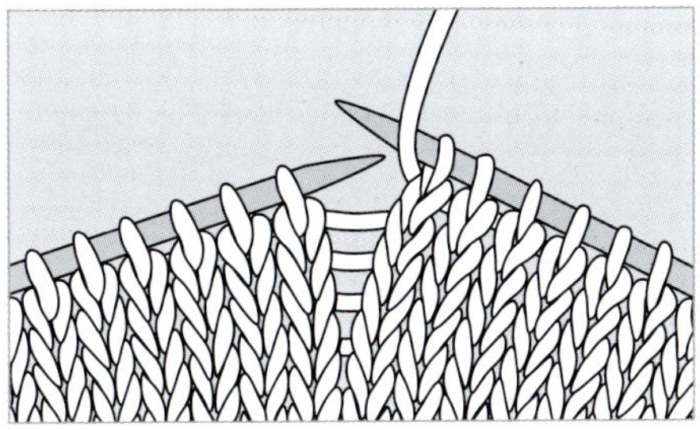

Knit In Front & Back

(abbreviated kfb)

Knit the next stitch but do **not** slip the old stitch off the left needle *(Fig. 5a)*. Insert the right needle into the **back** loop of the **same** stitch and knit it *(Fig. 5b)*, then slip the old stitch off the left needle.

Fig. 5a

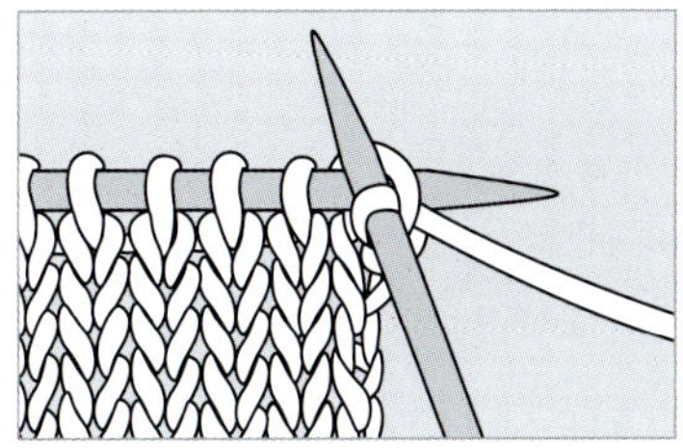

Fig. 5b

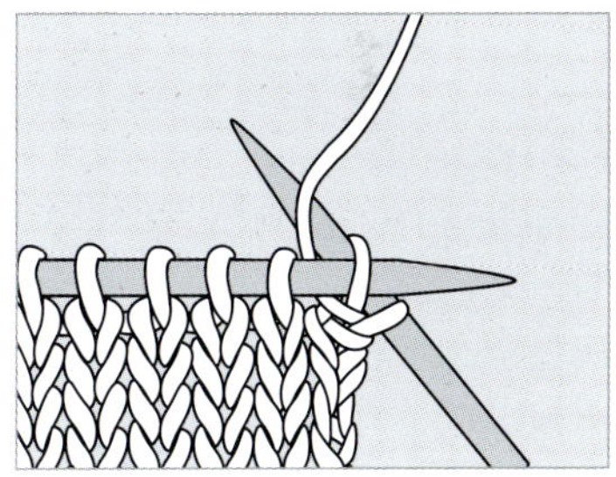

DECREASES

Knit 2 Together

(abbreviated K2 tog)

Insert the right needle into the **front** of the first two stitches on the left needle as if to **knit** ***(Fig. 6)***, then **knit** them together as if they were one stitch.

Fig. 6

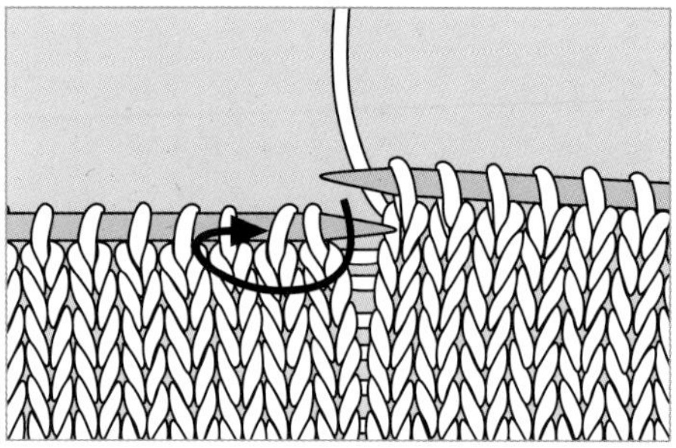

Purl 2 Together

(abbreviated P2 tog)

Insert the right needle into the **front** of the first two stitches on the left needle as if to **purl** ***(Fig. 7)***, then **purl** them together as if they were one stitch.

Fig. 7

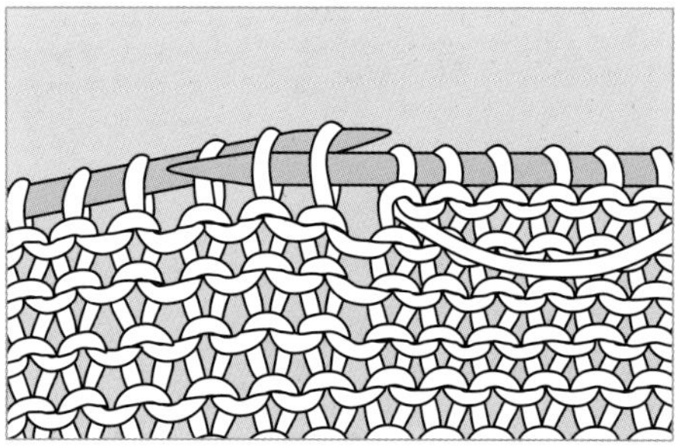

Slip, Slip, Knit *(abbreviated SSK)*

Separately slip two stitches as if to **knit** ***(Fig. 8a)***. Insert the left needle into the **front** of both slipped stitches ***(Fig. 8b)*** and then **knit** them together as if they were one stitch ***(Fig. 8c)***.

Fig. 8a

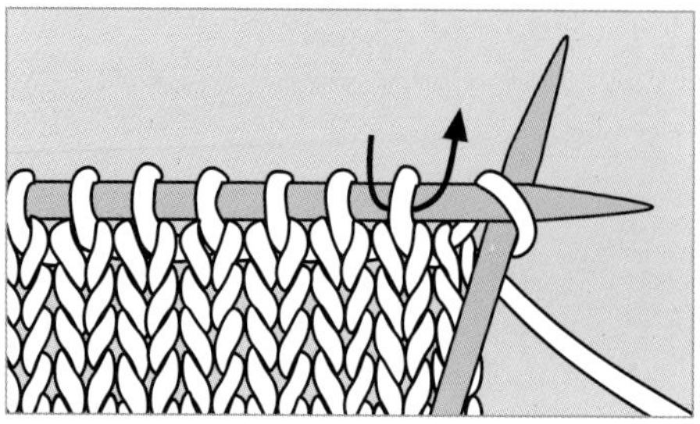

Fig. 8b

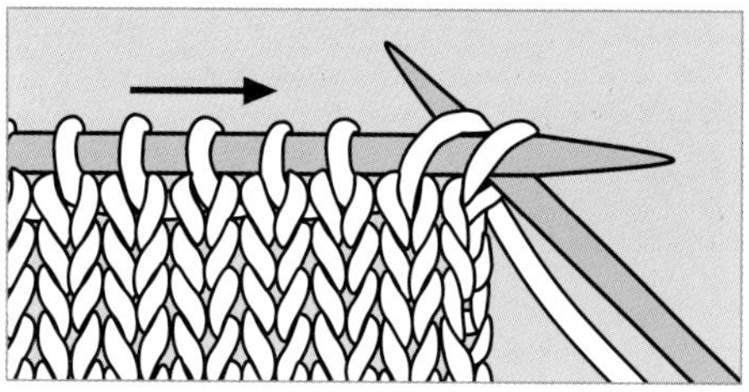

Fig. 8c

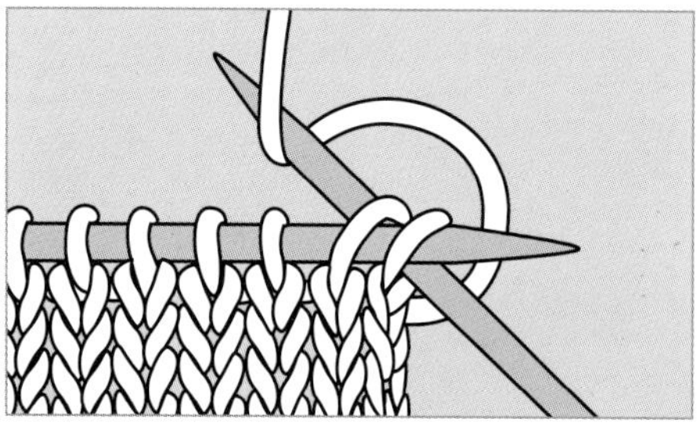

Slip 2 Together, Knit 1, Pass 2 Slipped Stitches Over

(abbreviated slip 2 tog, K1, P2SSO)

Slip two stitches together as if to **knit** ***(Fig. 9a)***, then knit the next stitch. With the left needle, bring both slipped stitches over the knit stitch ***(Fig. 9b)*** and off the needle.

Fig. 9a

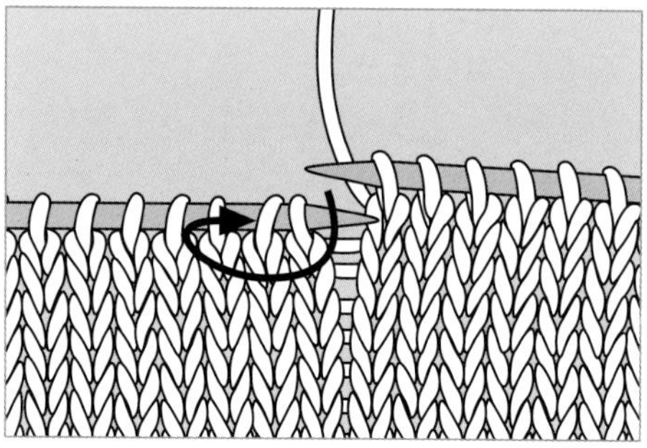

Fig. 9b

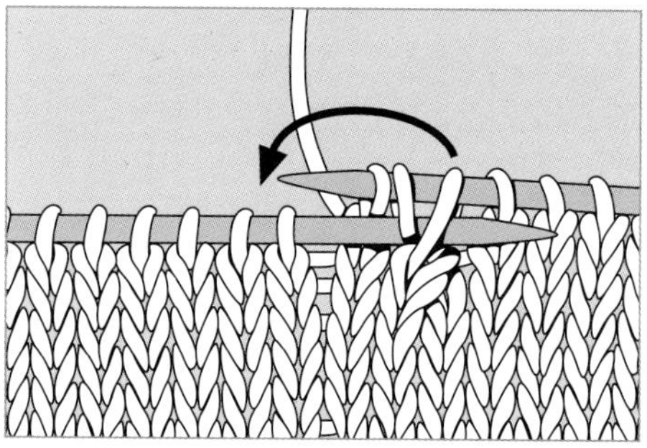

PICKING UP STITCHES

When instructed to pick up stitches, insert the needle from the **front** to the **back** under two strands at the edge of the worked piece ***(Figs. 10a & b)***. Put the yarn around the needle as if to **knit**, then bring the needle with the yarn back through the stitch to the right side, resulting in a stitch on the needle.

Fig. 10a

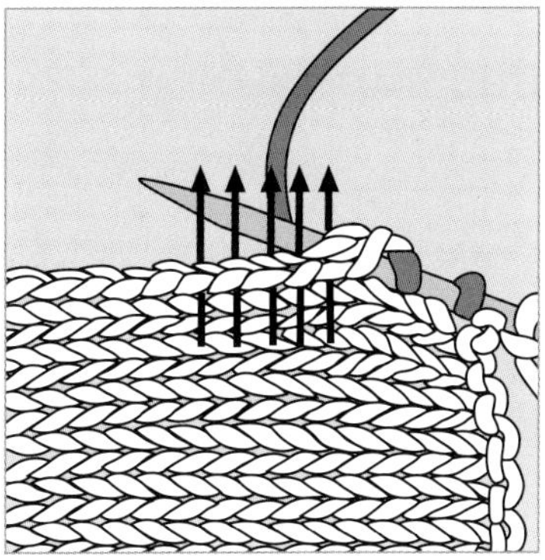

Fig. 10b

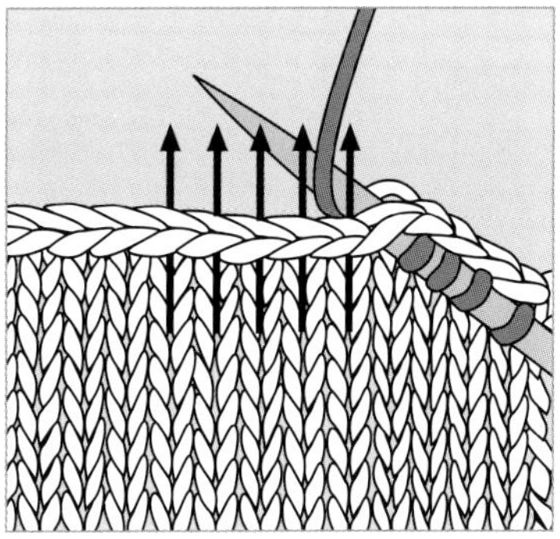

FRINGE

Cut a piece of cardboard 4" (10 cm) wide and half a long as specified in individual instructions for strands. Wind the yarn **loosely** and **evenly** around the cardboard lengthwise until the card if filled, then cut across one end; repeat as needed.

Hold together as many strands as specified in individual instructions; fold in half.

With **wrong** side facing and using a crochet hook, draw the folded end up through a stitch and pull the loose ends through the folded end ***(Fig. 11a)***; draw the knot up **tightly** ***(Fig. 11b)***. Repeat, spacing as specified in individual instructions.

Lay flat on a hard surface and trim the ends.

Fig. 11a

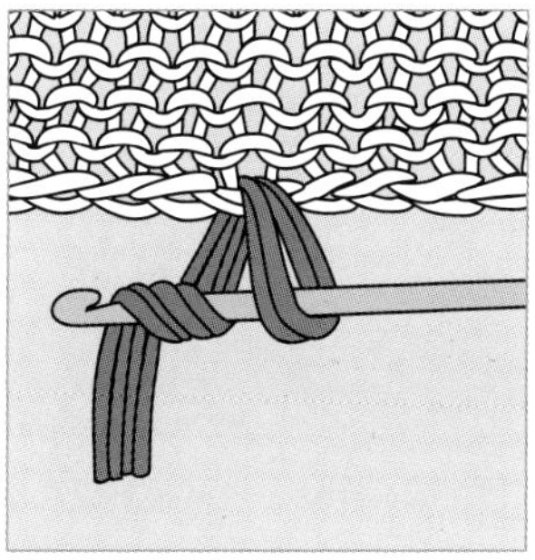

Fig. 11b

TASSEL

Cut a piece of cardboard 4" (10 cm) wide and half as long as specified in individual instructions for strands. Wind the yarn **loosely** and **evenly** around the cardboard lengthwise the number of times indicated in individual instructions. Cut an 18" (45.5 cm) length of yarn and insert it under all of the strands at the top of the cardboard; pull up **tightly** and tie securely. Leave the yarn ends long enough to attach the tassel. Cut the yarn at the opposite end of the cardboard and then remove it ***(Fig. 12a)***. Cut a 12" (30.5 cm) length of yarn and wrap it **tightly** around the tassel twice, 1" (2.5 cm) below the top ***(Fig. 12b)***; tie securely. Trim the ends.

Fig. 12a

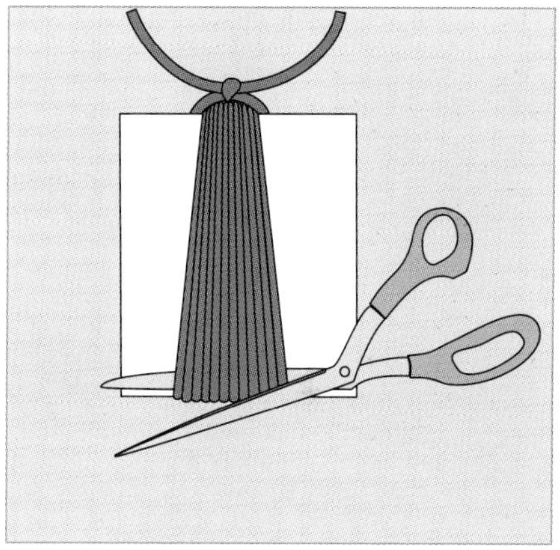

Fig. 12b

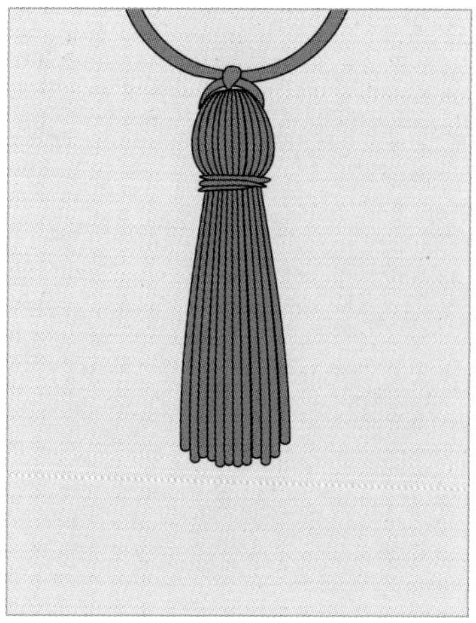

POM-POM

Cut a piece of cardboard 4" (10 cm) wide and as long as you want the diameter of your finished pom-pom to be.
Wind the yarn around the caredboard until it is approximately 1" (2.5 cm) thick in the middle ***(Fig. 13a)***. Carefully slip the yarn off the cardboard and firmly tie an 18" (45.5 cm) length of yarn around the middle ***(Fig. 13b)***. Leave yarn ends long enough to attach the pom-pom. Cut the loops on both ends and trim the pom-pom into a smooth ball ***(Fig. 13c)***.

Fig. 13a

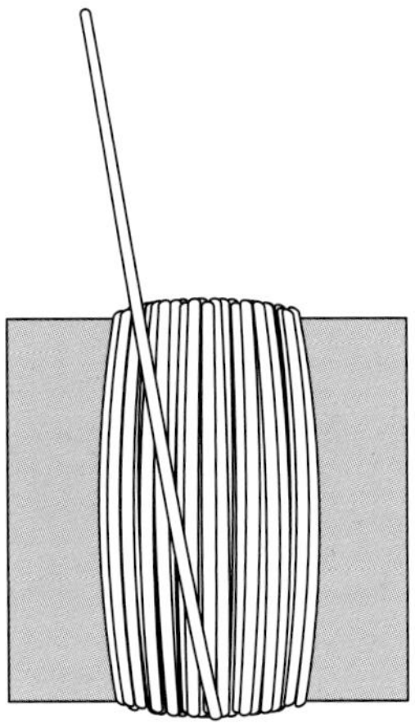

Fig. 13b

Fig. 13c

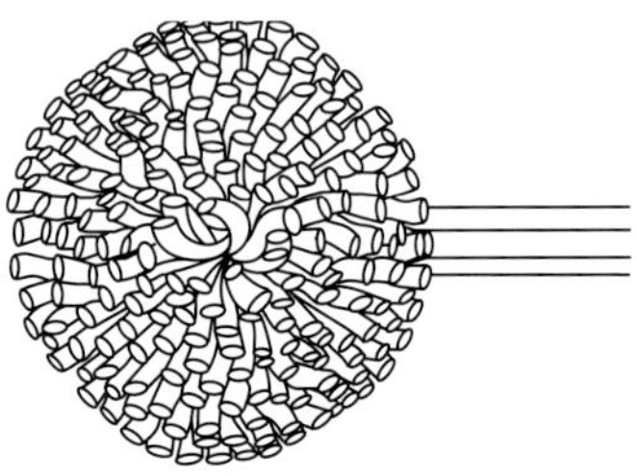

YARN INFORMATION

The items in this book were made using Lion Brand® Thick & Quick® a Super Bulky Weight yarn. Any brand of Super Bulky Weight yarn may be used. It is best to refer to the yardage/meters when determining how many balls or skeins to purchase. Remember, to achieve the finished size, it is the GAUGE/TENSION that is important, not the brand of yarn.

For your convenience, listed below are the yarn colors used to create out photography models. Because yarn manufacturers make frequent changes to their product lines, you may sometimes find it necessary to use a substitute yarn or to search for the discontinued product at alternate suppliers (locally or online).

LATVIAN BRAID COWL
#154 Grey Marble
#099 Fisherman
#155 Obsidian

BLANKET BASKET
#124 Barley

EYELET STRIPED WRAP
#099 Fisherman

WALL HANGING
#158 Mustard

MOSS COCOON CARDIGAN
#123 Oatmeal

CRISSCROSS CABLE PONCHO
#149 Charcoal

GARTER PYRAMID BLANKET
#148 Slate

TWIST FRONT HEADBAND
#148 Slate

LINEN SCARF
#149 Charcoal
#505 Marble

LOOPY PILLOWCASE
#123 Oatmeal

RIBBED TAM
#151 Graphite

SLOUCHY TOTE
#536 Fossil

Library of Congress Control Number: 2019940084

Made in China

Production Team: Instructional/Technical Editor - Linda A. Daley; Senior Graphic Artist - Lora Puls; Photo Stylist - Lori Wenger; and Photographer - Jason Masters.